Oswald Chambers' Publications

DISCIPLES INDEED

Oswald Chambers

OSWALD CHAMBERS' PUBLICATIONS
ASSOCIATION

and

NOVA PUBLISHING LTD

This edition copyright © 1955 by Oswald
Chambers' Publications Association Ltd and
Published 1991 by Nova Publishing Ltd,
29 Milber Industrial Estate, Newton Abbot
TQ12 4SG

First published 1955
First paperback edition 1973
Reprinted 1975, 1979, 1981
This printing 1991

ISBN 0 906330 36 X

Production & Printing in England by
NUPRINT LIMITED
Station Road, Harpenden, Herts AL5 4SE

CONTENTS

FOREWORD

Oswald Chambers was above all else a teacher of spiritual truth. Our Ascended Lord's promise was to give His Church 'some to be...teachers: for the perfecting of the saints' (Eph 4:11). This book contains messages spoken by such a teacher, full of wisdom and instruction in righteousness. Teachers call for learners. Some of us who heard the spoken word became humble and eager learners. Many who never saw or heard the speaker are learning from him now. In a recent letter the writer says, 'It is not generally known how these books came into being, and the time seems favourable for revealing God's providence in it all.' Oswald Chambers received his home-call in 1917 when working with the YMCA among the troops in Egypt. It seemed like the end of a fruitful ministry. Then it was that Mrs Chambers realised that her custom of taking down in shorthand her husband's lectures and addresses for her own profit had left her with a great store of spiritual wisdom which could be shared with the wider world by the printed page. So began a remarkable ministry of spreading in book form the original spoken words. As the writer of the above-mentioned letter says, 'The whole matter is a sheer miracle, especially as the only planning has been God's.'

Disciples Indeed speaks for itself. Other volumes

show by the outlines and headings given what careful preparation was made for every spoken message. But often the spontaneous word of a Spirit-filled man, whether the subject was Christian Doctrine, Psychology, Biblical Ethics or Homiletics, would be added, and appear in the shorthand notes. Many of these not included in the earlier publications are printed here. They touch a wide range of subjects, and take us to the heart of Oswald Chambers' message. They make this book a kind of *vade mecum* of sainthood.

David Lambert

ONE

BELIEF

*T*HE ONLY NOBLE sense in which we can claim to believe a thing is when we ourselves are living in the inner spirit of that thing.

I have no right to say I believe in God unless I order my life as under His all-seeing eye.

I have no right to say I believe that Jesus is the Son of God unless in my personal life I yield myself to that eternal Spirit, free from all self-seeking, which became incarnate in Jesus.

I have no right to say that I believe in forgiveness as an attribute of God if in my own heart I cherish an unforgiving temper. The forgiveness of God is the test by which I myself am judged.

Belief is a wholesale committal, it means making things inevitable, cutting off every possible retreat. Belief is as irrevocable as bereavement (cf. 2 Sam 12:21–3).

Belief is the abandonment of all claim to merit. That is why it is so difficult to believe.

A believer is one whose whole being is based on the finished work of redemption.

It is easier to be true to our convictions than to Jesus Christ, because if we are going to be true to Him our convictions will need to be altered.

Where we blunder is in trying to expound the cross doctrinally while refusing to do what Jesus told us to do, viz, lift Him up. 'And I, if I be lifted up from the earth, will draw all men unto Myself' (Jn 12:32, RV).

We are not sent to specialise in doctrine, but to lift up Jesus, and He will do the work of saving and sanctifying souls. When we become doctrine-mongers God's power is not known, only the passionateness of an individual appeal.

God has a way of bringing in facts which upset a man's doctrines if these stand in the way of God getting at his soul.

Doctrine is never the guide into Christian experience; doctrine is the exposition of Christian experience.

The further we get away from Jesus the more dogmatic we become over what we call our religious beliefs, while the nearer we live to Jesus the less we have of certitude and the more of confidence in Him.

You cannot understand Jesus Christ unless you accept the New Testament revelation of Him, you must be biased for Him before you can understand Him.

Beware of coming to Jesus with preconceived notions of your own, come relying on the Holy Spirit. *'He shall glorify Me,'* said Jesus (Jn 16:13–14).

Once allow that Jesus Christ is all the New Testament proclaims Him to be, and you are borne on irresistibly to believe that what He says about Himself is true.

The most conspicuous thing in the New Testament is the supremacy given to our Lord; to-day the supremacy is apt to be given to phases of the truth, to doctrines, and not to Jesus Christ.

Truth is a person, not a proposition; if I pin my faith to a logical creed I will be disloyal to the Lord Jesus.

The most fundamental heresies which split the

Christian Church are those built on what Jesus Christ can do instead of on Himself. Wreckage in spiritual experience always follows.

Many a man spurns Jesus Christ in any phase other than that of his particular religious idea.

Every partial truth has so much error in it that you can dispute it, but you can't dispute 'truth as it is in Jesus'.

Watch the things you say you can't believe, and then recall the things you accept without thinking, eg your own existence.

It is impossible to prove a fact, facts have to be swallowed, and the man who swallows revelation facts is no more of a fool than the man who swallows common-sense facts on the evidence of his senses. Face facts, and play the sceptic with explanations.

The 'ever-learning-and-never-able-to-come-to-the-knowledge-of-the-truth' stage is the cause of all spiritual epidemics; we won't realise what God has revealed.

You can't unveil truth when you like; when the unveiling comes, beware. That moment marks your going back or your going on.

Truth is of the implicit order, you can't define truth, and yet every man is so constituted that at times his longing for truth is insatiable. It is not sufficient to remain with a longing for truth, because there is something at the basis of things which drives a man to the truth if he is honest.

When a man says he can't believe, don't argue with him on what he doesn't believe but ask him what he does believe, and proceed from that point; disbelief as often arises from temperament as from sin. Every man believes in a good character, then refer to Jesus Christ as the best character in history, and ask him to believe that what He says is likely to be true (eg Lk 11:13; Jn 3:16), and get him to transact business on that.

When once you come in contact with Jesus you are not conscious of any effort to believe in Him.

If I believe the character of Jesus, am I living up to what I believe?

The danger of pietistic movements is that we are told what we must feel, and we can't get near God because we are so hopelessly dependent on pious attitudes, consequently what is seen is not the New Testament stamp of saint, but the mixture of an insubordinate intellect along with an affected clinging to Jesus with devotion.

Whenever a holiness movement raises its head and begins to be conscious of its own holiness, it is liable to become an emissary of the devil, although it started with an emphasis on a neglected truth.

We must continually take stock of what is ours in Christ Jesus because only in that way will we understand what God intends us to be.

If you preach holiness, or sanctification, or divine healing, or the second coming, you are off the track because you de-centralise the truth. We have to fix our eyes on Jesus Christ, not on what He does. *'I am the Truth.'*

If I am going to know who Jesus is, I must obey Him. The majority of us don't know Jesus because we have not the remotest intention of obeying Him.

Our deadliest temptations are not so much those that destroy Christian belief as those that corrupt and destroy the Christian temper.

The great paralysis of our heart is unbelief. Immediately I view anything as inevitable about any human being, I am an unbeliever.

There is a difference between believing God and believing about Him, you are always conscious of the latter, it makes you a prig. If by letting your beliefs go you get hold of God Himself, let them go.

Beware of worshipping Jesus as the Son of God, and professing your faith in Him as the Saviour of the world, while you blaspheme Him by the complete evidence in your daily life that He is powerless to do anything in and through you.

The greatest challenge to a Christian is to believe Matthew 28:18 — *'All power is given unto Me in heaven and in earth.'* How many of us get into a panic when we are faced by physical desolation, by death, or war, injustice, poverty, disease? All these in all their force will never turn to panic the one who believes in the absolute sovereignty of his Lord.

TWO

THE BIBLE

'*T*HE WORD' IS Jesus Himself (Jn 1:1), therefore we must have an experimental knowledge of Him before we understand the literal words of the Bible.

The danger to-day is that people are being nourished not with the Bible so much as with conceptions which ignore Jesus Christ.

Bible facts are either revelation facts or nonsense. It depends on me which they are to me.

God does not thunder His truth into our ears, our attitude of mind must be submissive to revelation facts. Each one of us brings certain prejudices, civilised pre-judgements, which greatly hinder our understanding of revelation facts.

Our attitude to the Bible is a stupid one; we come to the Bible for proof of God's existence, but the Bible has no meaning for us until we know God does exist. The Bible states and affirms facts for the benefit of those who believe in God; those who don't believe in God can tear it to bits if they choose.

People can dispute the words of the Bible as they like, but get a soul in whom the craving for God has come, and the words of the Bible create the new life in him. '*...being born again,...by the word of God*' (1 Pet 1:23).

If we understood what happens when we use the

Word of God, we would use it oftener. The disablement of the devil's power by means of the Word of God conveyed through the lips of a servant of His, is inconceivable.

The main characteristic which is the proof of the indwelling Spirit is an amazing tenderness in personal dealing, and a blazing truthfulness with regard to God's Word.

There is no true illumination apart from the written Word. Spiritual impressions generated from my own experience are of no importance, and if I pay attention to them I will pay no attention to the words of Jesus.

The test of God's truth is that it fits you exactly; if it does not, question whether it is His truth.

Beware of bartering the Word of God for a more suitable conception of your own.

Every impulse must wed itself to the express statements of the Bible, otherwise they will lead astray.

The thing to ask yourself is, 'Does the Bible say it?' not, 'I don't think that is a good view of God.'

Profoundly speaking, it is not sufficient to say, 'Because God says it,' or, 'Because the Bible says it,' unless you are talking to people who know God and know the Bible to be His Word. If you appeal from the authority of God or of the Bible to a man not born again, he will pay no attention to you because he does not stand on the same platform. You have to find a provisional platform on which he can stand with you, and in the majority of cases you will find that the platform is that of moral worth. If Jesus Christ is proved worthy on the plane men are on, they will be ready to put Him as the most worthy One, and all the rest will follow.

Whenever human nature gets driven to the end of things the Bible is the only Book, and God the only Being, in the world.

The reason some of us are not healthy spiritually is because we don't use the Bible as the Word of God but only as a text-book.

Beware of making a fetish of a word God once spoke to you; if you stick to the word God spoke you will leave Him, and the result is harshness and stagnation, a refusal to budge from the precedent you have established.

Watch every time the Word of God is made a sacrament to you through someone else, it will make you re-tune your ears to His Word.

There are saints who are being rattled out of holiness by fussy work for God, whereas one five minutes of brooding on God's truth would do more good than all their work of fuss.

It is what the Bible imparts to us that is of value.

The Bible does not thrill, the Bible nourishes. Give time to the reading of the Bible and the recreating effect is as real as that of fresh air physically.

If I have disobeyed, the Word of God is dried up, there is 'no open vision'. Immediately I obey the Word is poured in.

To read the Bible according to God's providential order in your circumstances is the only way to read it, viz., in the blood and passion of personal life.

The statements of Scripture apart from the Holy Spirit's illumination are dull; it needs no spiritual insight to regard Jesus Christ as a Man who lived beyond His time, but when I am born again I have insight into the Person of Jesus, an insight that comes through communion with God by means of the Bible.

Beware of interpreting Scripture in order to make it suit a pre-arranged doctrine of your own.

Exegesis is not torturing a text to agree with a theory of my own, but leading out its meaning.

Beware of reasoning about God's Word, obey it.

An absurd thing to say is — 'Give me a text to prove it.' You cannot give a text to prove any one of God's revelations, you can only give a text to prove your simplification of those revelations. A text-proof is generally used to bolster up a personal spiritual affinity of my own.

We are to be servants and handmaids of the Gospel, not devotees of the Bible, then God can make us living mediums whereby His Word becomes a sacrament to others.

THREE

THE CALL OF GOD

*I*F YOU ONLY know what God can do your talk is altogether of that, a logical exposition of doctrine, but if you have heard God's call you will always keep to the one centre, the Person of the Lord Jesus Christ.

Discard any emotion or call to work which cannot find itself at home in the absolute mastery of Jesus Christ.

If I hear the call of God and refuse to obey, I become the dullest, most common-place of Christians because I have seen and heard and refused to obey.

No experience on earth is sufficient to be taken as a call of God; you must know that the call is from God for whom you care more than for all your experiences; then nothing can daunt you.

You can never fag the life out of the one whose service springs from listening to the voice of God, its inspiration is drawn not from human sympathy, but from God Himself.

The Call is the inner motive of having been gripped by God — spoilt for every aim in life saving that of disciplining men to Jesus.

One man or woman called of God is worth a hundred who have elected to work for God.

It is an erroneous notion that you have to wait for

the call of God: see that you are in such a condition that you can realise it (Is 6:8).

If God has called any man or woman in this College into His service, as He undoubtedly has, never allow anyone to interfere with your obedience to His call. Let God do what He likes, He knows exactly where you are, and when the time is fit to make you broken bread in His hands.

We need no call of God to help our fellow men, that is the natural call of humanity; but we do need the supernatural work of God's grace before we are fit for God to help Himself through us.

If a man is called to preach the Gospel, God will crush him till the light of the eye, the power of the life, the ambition of the heart, is all riveted on Himself. That is not done easily. It is not a question of saintliness, it has to do with the Call of God.

FOUR

THE CHARACTER OF GOD

'NO MAN HATH seen God at any time; the only begotten Son, which is in the bosom of the Father, He hath declared Him' (Jn 1:18). A Christian accepts all he knows about God on the authority of Jesus Christ; he can find out nothing about God by his own unaided intellect.

The God I infer by my common sense has no power over me at all.

The vindication of God to our intelligence is the most difficult process. Only when we see righteousness and justice exhibited in the Person of Jesus Christ can we vindicate God.

In the face of problems as they are, we see in Jesus Christ an exhibition of where our faith is to be placed, viz., in a God whose ways we do not understand.

Jesus Christ reveals, not an embarrassed God, not a confused God, not a God who stands apart from the problems, but One who stands in the thick of the whole thing with man.

When a so-called rationalist points out sin and iniquity and disease and death, and says, 'How does God answer that?' you have always a fathomless answer — the Cross of Christ.

God's ways are 'past finding out!' We often state the character of God in terms of brutal harshness while our motive is to glorify Him.

Never accept an explanation that travesties God's character.

There are some questions God cannot answer until you have been brought by obedience to be able to stand the answer. Be prepared to suspend your judgement until you have heard God's answer for yourself.

There *is* a dark line in God's face, but what we do know about Him is so full of peace and joy that we can wait for His interpretation.

God's order is clearly marked out in the first and the last; His permissive will is seen in the process in between where everything is disorganised because of sin. The Christian is one who by the power of the indwelling Spirit sees the final issue.

The Psalmist was perplexed when he saw 'the prosperity of the wicked...' (Ps 73:1–12); God's final purpose is holiness, holy men and women, and He restrains none of the forces which go against that purpose.

Beware lest your attitude to God's truth reminds Him that He is very unwise. Everything worth while in life is dangerous, and yet we would have God such a tepid Being that He runs no risks!

Believe what you do believe and stick to it, but don't profess to believe more than you intend to stick to. If you say you believe God is love, stick to it, though all Providence becomes a pandemonium shouting that God is cruel to allow what He does.

Never attempt to explain God to an exasperated soul, because you cannot. Don't take the part of Job's friends and say you can explain the whole thing; if you think you can, you are very shallow. You have to take on the attitude of vicarious waiting till God brings the light.

Remember, each life has a solitary way alone with God. Be reverent with His ways in dealing with other souls because you have no notion, any more than Job had, why things are as they are. Most of us are much too desirous of getting hold of a line which will vindicate us in our view of God.

It is perilously possible to make our conceptions of God like molten lead poured into a specially designed mould, and when it is cold and hard we fling it at the heads of the religious people who don't agree with us.

God is true to the laws of His own nature, not to my way of expounding how He works.

We have to get out of the old pagan way of guiding ourselves by our heads and get into the Christian way of being guided by faith in a personal God, whose methods are a perpetual contradiction to our every preconceived notion.

We only see another in the light of what we think he is, it takes an amount of surgery on the inside to make us see other people as they really are, and it is the same with what we think about God; we take the facts revealed in the Bible and try to fit them into our own ideas of what God is like.

Am I becoming more and more in love with God as a holy God, or with the conception of an amiable Being who says, 'Oh well, sin doesn't matter much'?

God never coerces, neither does He ever accommodate His demands to human compromise, and we are disloyal to Him if we do.

Watch the margins of your mind when you begin to take the view that it doesn't matter whether God is holy or not; it is the beginning of being a traitor to Jesus Christ.

Spiritual insight does not so much enable us to understand God as to understand that He is at work in the ordinary things of life, in the ordinary stuff human nature is made of.

Learn to give honour to God when good works are

done, but also learn to discern whether or not they are done by God's servants. The most outrageous moment for the devil will be when he finds that in spite of himself he has done God's will; and the same with the man who has been serving his own ends.

Everything the devil does, God over-reaches to serve His own purpose.

Have I ever had a glimpse of this — that God would not be altered if all our civilised life went to pieces?

Over-refinement in civilisation turns God's order upside down.

God has no respect for our civilisations because He did not found them. While civilisation is not God's, it is His providential protection for men, generally restraining the bad, and affording His children the means of developing their life in Him.

When the present phase is over God won't have elbow-room, it will be all insurance and combine, and God won't be able to get in anywhere. What is true of civilisation will be true of us individually unless we remember to put God first.

In a time of calamity God appears to pay scant courtesy to all our art and culture, He sweeps the whole thing aside till civilisation rages at Him. It is 'the babe' and 'the fool' who get through in the day of God's visitation.

God cannot come to me in any way but His own way, and His way is often insignificant and unobtrusive.

Never accept an explanation of any of God's ways which involves what you would scorn as false and unfair in a man.

God does not act according to His own precedents, therefore logic or a vivid past experience can never take the place of a personal faith in a personal God.

God never crushes men beneath the fear of judgement without revealing the possibility of victorious virtue.

We say that God foresaw sin, and made provision for it: the Bible revelation is that 'the Lamb that hath been slain from the foundation of the world' is the exact expression of the nature of God.

FIVE

EXPERIENCE

*E*XPERIENCES ARE APT to be exalted out of all due measure whereas they are but the outward manifestation of the oneness with God made possible for us in Christ Jesus.

Get into the habit of chasing yourself out of the sickly morbid experiences that are not based on having been with Jesus (see Acts 4:13); they are not only valueless, but excessively dangerous.

The great bedrock of Christian experience is the outside fact of the Resurrection made inwardly real by the incoming of the Holy Spirit. 'That I may know Him, and the power of His resurrection, . . .' (Phil 3:10).

If your experience is not worthy of the Risen, Ascended Christ, then fling it overboard.

Whenever ecstasies or visions of God unfit us for practical life they are danger signals that the life is on the wrong track.

Our identity with Jesus Christ is immediately practical or not at all, that is, the new identity must manifest itself in our mortal flesh otherwise we can easily hoax ourselves into delusions. Being 'made the righteousness of God in Him' is the most powerfully practical experience in a human life.

Insubordination characterises much of what is called 'The Higher Christian Life'; it is spiritual anarchy, based on *my* intuitions, *my* private interpretations, *my* experiences, while refusing to submit to the words of the Lord Jesus.

My experience of salvation never constitutes me an expounder of the Atonement. I am always apt to take my experience for an inclusive interpretation instead of its being merely a gateway for *me* into salvation.

We continually want to present our understanding of how God has worked in our own experience, consequently we confuse people. Present Jesus Christ, lift Him up, and the Holy Spirit will do in them what He has done in you.

A great deal of what we have to proclaim can never be experienced, but whenever God's standard is presented we are either exonerated or condemned by the way we ourselves carry out the dictates of the Holy Spirit.

Experience as an end in itself is a disease; experience as a result of the life being based on God is health.

Spiritual famine and dearth, if it does not start from sin, starts from dwelling entirely on the experience God gave me instead of on God who gave me the experience.

When I plant my faith on the Lord Jesus my experiences don't make me conscious of them, they produce in me the life of a child.

If my experience makes anyone wish to emulate me, I am decoying that one away from God.

'Because I have had more experience of life than you have, therefore I can discern God's will better than you can.' Not at all. Whenever I put my experience of life, or my intelligence, or anything other than dependence on God, as the ground of understanding the will of God I rob Him of glory.

It is on the line of impulse that Satan leads the saints astray, in spite of Jesus Christ's warning — 'so as to lead astray, if possible, even the elect.' It is spiritual impulse that leads off at a tangent. Satan does not come as 'an angel of light' to anybody but a saint.

Whenever we get light from God on a particular phase we incline to limit God's working to that phase, forgetting that we cannot tie up Almighty God to anything built up out of our own experience.

One man's experience is as valuable as another's, but experience has nothing to do with facts. Facts pay no attention to us, facts have to be accepted, they are the real autocrats in life.

You cannot deal with facts as you like, you may object to them, but a fact is a fact, whether a common-sense fact or a revelation fact.

In spiritual experience it is not your intellect that guides you; intellect illuminates what is yours, and you get a thrill of delight because you recognise what you have been going through but could not state.

Whenever the Bible refers to facts of human experience, look to your experience for the answer; when the Bible refers to standards of revelation, look to God, not to your experience.

Beware of making your religious experiences a cloak for a lack of reality.

If you have been going on with God you find He has knocked the bottom-board out of your fanaticism; where you used to be narrow and bigoted, you now exhibit His Spirit.

Would to God we got finished once for all with the experience of being adjusted to God, and let Him send us forth into vicarious service for Him!

THE HOLY SPIRIT

*I*T IS NOT what we feel, or what we know, but ever what we *receive* from God — and a fool can receive a gift. 'If ye then, being evil, know how to give good gifts unto your children, how much more shall your heavenly Father give the Holy Spirit to them that ask Him?' (Lk 11:13). It is so simple that everyone who is not simple misses it.

Beware of telling people they must be worthy to receive the Holy Spirit; you can't be worthy, you must know you are unworthy, then you will ask for the gift — 'If ye then, *being evil…*'

The biggest blessing in your life was when you came to the end of trying to be a Christian, the end of reliance on natural devotion, and were willing to come as a pauper and receive the Holy Spirit. The humiliation is that we have to be quite sure we need Him, so many of us are quite sure we don't need Him.

It is extraordinary how things fall off from a man like autumn leaves once he comes to the place where there is no rule but that of the personal domination of the Holy Spirit.

We continually want to substitute our transactions with God for the great mystic powerful work of the Holy Spirit. 'The wind bloweth where it listeth, and thou hearest the voice thereof, but knowest not whence it cometh and whither it goeth: *so is every one that is born of the Spirit*' (Jn 3:8, RV).

By regeneration we are put into right relationship with God, then we have the same human nature, working on the same lines, but with a different driving power expressing itself, so that the 'members' which were used for the wrong are now used for the good (see Romans 6:17–21).

The strenuous effort of the saint is not to produce holiness, but to express in actual circumstances the disposition of the Son of God which is imparted to him by the Holy Ghost.

Beware of seeking power rather than the personal relationship to Jesus Christ which is the grand avenue through which the Holy Spirit comes in His working power. 'But ye shall receive power, when the Holy Ghost is come upon you; *and ye shall be My witnesses*' (Acts 1:8).

The message of Pentecost is an emphasis, not on the Holy Ghost, but on the Risen and Ascended Christ (Jn 16:13–15).

The Holy Spirit takes care that we fix our attention on Jesus Christ; then He will look after the presentation given of our Lord through us.

Devotion to Jesus is the expression of the Holy Spirit's work in me.

The Holy Spirit is concerned only with glorifying Jesus, not with glorifying our human generosities.

The deep and engrossing need of those of us who name the Name of Christ is reliance on the Holy Spirit.

Jesus Christ reinstates us to the position lost through sin (see Romans 5:12); we come at this knowledge experimentally, but it is never our understanding of salvation that leads to salvation. Salvation is *experienced* first, then to understand it needs the work of the Holy Spirit, which is surprising and incalculable.

We 'become partakers of the divine nature' by receiving the Holy Ghost who sheds abroad the love of God in our hearts (Rom 5:5), and the oneness is manifested in a life of abandon and obedience — both unconscious.

If you are being checked by the Holy Spirit over a wrong thing you are allowing in yourself, beware of only captiously seeing the limitations in other people; you will diverge further away from God if you don't recognise that it is the still small voice of God *to you*.

There is nothing so still and gentle as the checks of the Holy Spirit; if they are yielded to, emancipation is the result; but let them be trifled with, and there will come a hardening of the life away from God. Don't 'quench the Spirit'.

There is no room for harsh judgement on the part of a child of God. Harsh judgement is based, not on the sternness of the Holy Ghost, but on my refusal to bear someone else's burden.

Beware of everything in which you have to justify yourself to yourself because the underlying fact is that you have cajoled yourself into taking a decision born of temperamental convictions instead of in entire reliance on the Holy Spirit.

The inspiration of the Holy Spirit is not an impulse to make me act but to enable me to interpret God's meaning; if I do act on the impulse of the inspiration, it is a mere physical reaction in myself. Impulse is God's knock at my door that He might come in, not for me to open the door and go out.

The salvation of Jesus Christ makes a man's personality intense; very few of us are real until the Holy Spirit gets hold of us.

The Holy Spirit does not obliterate a man's personality; He lifts it to its highest use, viz., for the portrayal of the Mind of God.

Beware of the 'show business' — 'I want to be baptised with the Holy Ghost so that I may do wonderful works.' God never allows anyone to do wonderful works: *He* does them, and the baptism of the Holy Ghost prevents my seeing them in order to glory in them.

'When He ascended on high…He gave gifts unto men' (Eph 4:8; cf Acts 2:33). The only sign that a particular gift is from the Ascended Christ is that it edifies the Church. Much of our Christian work to-day is built on what the Apostle pleads it should not be built on, viz., the excellencies of the natural virtues.

Be careful to notice the difference between an offended personal prejudice which makes you feel ruffled and huffy, and the intuitive sense of bondage produced by the Holy Spirit when you are listening to something that is not God's truth.

We must distinguish between the bewilderment arising from conviction of sin and the bewilderment arising from confusion in thinking; the latter is the inevitable result in a traditionally Christian mind on first receiving the Holy Spirit; but a curious thing to note is that a heathen mind experiences no such bewilderment on receiving the Holy Spirit because there are no preconceived notions to be got rid of.

The mind that is not produced by obedience to the Holy Spirit in the final issue hates God.

If you are in danger of building on the natural virtues, which are a remnant of the former creation, the Holy Spirit will throw a searchlight and show you things that cause you to shudder. He will reveal a vindictiveness, a maliciousness, you never knew before.

Let God bring you through some midnight, when

the Holy Spirit reminds you of what you once were, of your religious hypocrisies — the things the devil whispers you should forget; let God bring you to the dust before Him. This experience will always come in the path of those God is going to take up into His purposes.

The baptism of the Holy Ghost means the extinction of life-fires that are not of God, and everything becomes instinct with the life of God.

The Holy Spirit is the One who regenerates us into the Family to which Jesus Christ belongs, until by the eternal efficacy of the Cross we are made partakers of the Divine nature.

The Holy Spirit is not a substitute for Jesus. The Holy Spirit is all that Jesus was, made real in personal experience *now*.

There is one thing we cannot imitate: we cannot imitate being full of the Holy Ghost.

The mark of the Holy Spirit in a man's life is that he has gone to his own funeral and the thought of himself never enters.

The sign that the Holy Spirit is being obeyed by me is that I am not dominated by my sensualities. 'And they that are of Christ have crucified the flesh with the passions and the lusts thereof' (Gal 5:24). Sensualities are not gross only, they can be very refined.

'What? know ye not that your body is the temple of the Holy Ghost which is in you...?' (1 Cor 6:19). The indwelling of the Holy Spirit is the climax of Redemption.

The great impelling power of the Holy Spirit is seen in its most fundamental working whenever an issue of will is pushed. It is pleasanter to listen to poetical discourses, more agreeable to have your affinities appealed to, but it is not good enough, it leaves you exactly as you were. The Gospel appeal comes with a stinging grip — 'Will you?', or, 'Won't you?' 'I will accept,' or, 'I'll put it off', — both are decisions, remember.

We have to distinguish between acquiring and receiving. We *acquire* habits of prayer and Bible reading, and we *receive* our salvation, we *receive* the Holy Spirit, we *receive* the grace of God. We give more attention to the things we acquire; all God pays attention to is what we receive. Those things we receive can never be taken from us because God holds those who receive His gifts.

The fruit of pseudo-evangelism is different from 'the fruit of the Spirit' (Gal 5:22–3).

Guard as your greatest gift the anointing of the Holy Spirit, viz., the right of access to God for yourself. 'And as for you, the anointing which ye received of Him abideth in you' (1 Jn 2:27).

It is the fine art of the Holy Spirit to be alone with God.

SEVEN

THE MORAL LAW

*I*T HAS BEEN a favourite belief in all ages that if only men were taught what good is, everyone would choose it; but history and human experience prove that that is not so. To know what good *is* is not to *be* good.

My conscience makes me know what I ought to do, but it does not empower me to do it. 'For that which I do I allow not; for what I would, that do I not; but what I hate, that do I' (Rom 7:15).

To say that if I am persuaded a thing is wrong I won't do it, is not true. The mutiny of human nature is that it will do it whether it is wrong or not.

The problem in practical experience is not to know what is right, but to do it. My natural spirit may know a great many things, but I never can be what I know I ought to be until I receive the Life which has life in itself, viz., the Holy Spirit. That is the practical working of the Redemption.

'Morality is altogether based on utilitarian standards': it is not, a man's conscience will come in every time when he doesn't want it to.

Conscience resides in the essential spirit of a man, not in his reasoning faculty; it is the one thing that assists a man in his unregenerate days.

Why are men not worse than they are? The reason is the existence of the moral law of God which restrains men in spite of the impulse towards wrong, consequently you find remnants of the strivings of the moral law where you least expect it because the moral law is independent entirely of the opposition to it on the part of individual men.

When God's law is presented beware of the proud self-confidence which says, 'This is good enough for me, I don't intend to soar any higher.'

In dealing with the question of disease both moral and physical, we must deal with it in the light of the Redemption. If you want to know how far wrong the world has got you learn it, not in a hospital, but at the Cross. We learn by what it cost God to redeem the world how criminally out of moral order the universe has got.

The guilt abroad to-day can never be dealt with by pressing a social ethic or a moral order, or by an enfolding sympathy for man, while pooh-poohing the demands of a holy God.

Very few of us know what *love of God* is, we know what *love of moral good* is, and the curious thing is that that leads us away from God more quickly than does a terror of moral evil; 'the good is ever the enemy of the best.'

Our lawlessness can be detected in relation to the words, 'Come unto Me.'

Liberty means ability not to violate the law; licence means personal insistence on doing what I like.

If a man is not holy, he is immoral; it does not matter how good he seems, immorality is at the basis of the whole thing. It may not show itself as immoral physically, but it will show itself as immoral in the sight of God (see Luke 16:15).

Intellectual scepticism is good, but a man is to blame for moral scepticism. Every man believes in goodness and uprightness and integrity until he perverts his taste by going wrong himself.

Beware of giving way to spiritual ecstasies, it disconnects you from the great ordinances of God and shakes the very basis of sane morality God has made.

There is no such thing as a *wrong* wrong, only a *right* that has gone wrong. Every error had its start in a truth, else it would have no power.

In the moral realm if you don't do things quickly, you will never do them. Never postpone a moral decision.

Second thoughts on moral matters are always deflections.

It is only when a moral act is performed and light thrown on realities that we understand the relationship between our human lives and the Cross of Christ.

EIGHT

PERSONALITY

NOTHING IN CONNECTION with our personality is so disastrously enervating as disillusionment about ourselves. We much prefer our own idea of ourselves to the stern realisation of what we really are. Paul warns, 'Let no man think of himself more highly than he ought to think.' Watch how God has disillusioned you over yourself and see the value of it for the future.

There is a difference between the reality of personality and its actuality, the latter is continually changing; you are sensitive now where you were indifferent before, and *vice versa*.

Individuality can never become a sacrament, it is only personality that can become a sacrament through oneness with Jesus Christ.

You often find people in the world are more desirable, easier to get on with, than people in the Kingdom. There is frequently a stubbornness, a self-opinionativeness, in Christians not exhibited by people in the world.

If there is to be another Revival it will be through the readjustment of those of us on the inside who call ourselves Christians.

It is obvious that as we have grown physically we have developed into more useful human beings, but have we grown finer morally and spiritually? grown more pure and holy? We may have become broader-minded and yet not be so fine in perception as we used to be. It takes a lot of self-scrutiny to know whether we are evolving all the time in every domain of our being. 'Therefore by their fruits ye shall know them.'

The greatest test of Christianity is the wear and tear of daily life, it is like the shining of silver, the more it is rubbed the brighter it grows.

It is well to remember that our examination of ourselves can never be unbiased or unprejudiced, so that we are only safe in taking the estimate of ourselves from our Creator instead of from our own introspection, whether conceited or depressed.

The modern Pharisee is the one who pretends to be the publican — 'Oh, I would never call myself a saint!' Exaggerated self-depreciation and exaggerated conceit are both diseased.

God has an alchemy of Providence by means of which our inner spirit precipitates itself — obliged to be holy if you are holy; obliged to be impure if you are impure. It is impossible to repress the ruling spirit when in the presence of the Spirit of God in another.

Crises reveal character. When we are put to the test the hidden resources of our character are revealed exactly.

We have to do more than we are built to do naturally; we have to do all the Almighty builds us to do.

The phrase 'Self-mastery' is profoundly wrong although practically correct. Profoundly, a man can never be master of what he does not understand, therefore the only master of a man is not himself, or another man, but God. 'Self-mastery' is correct if it means carrying out the edicts of God in myself.

Leave no subject connected with your own soul until you have landed at the door of the supernatural.

Natural resources are liable to break down in a crisis, but if your life is based on the supernatural God His power will manifest itself, and turn the moment that might have been tragic into triumph.

Unity of self is difficult to describe, it is the state in which there is no consciousness of myself, only of unity in myself. A false unity is fictitious because at any moment it may fall to pieces in an agony of remorse.

How long it takes for all the powers in a Christian to be at one depends on one thing only, viz., obedience.

The reason self-interest is detected in us is because there are whole tracts of our nature that have never been fused by the Spirit of God into one central purpose.

If all Jesus Christ came to do is to produce disunity in me He had better never have come, because I am created to have such harmony in myself that I am unconscious of it.

Self-complacency and spiritual pride are always the beginning of degeneration. When I begin to be satisfied with where I am spiritually, instantly I begin to degenerate.

There is no pride equal to spiritual pride, and no obstinacy equal to spiritual obstinacy, because they are nearest to the throne of God, and are most like the devil.

It is never our wicked heart that is the difficulty, but our obstinate will.

'Show me what to do and I'll do it' — you won't. It is easy to knock down one type of pride and erect another.

The only reason I can't get to God is pride, no matter how humble I seem.

When any personal position is credited by me to

myself, God's decree is that it hardens my heart in pride.

The only sacrifice acceptable to God is 'a broken and a contrite heart', not a moral upright life built on pride. When I stand on the basis of penitence, God's salvation is manifested immediately.

Note the thing which makes you say, 'I don't believe it,' it will prove where you are spiritually. What I resent reveals who governs me.

If excellence of character is made the test, the grace of God is 'made void', because a man can develop an amazing perfection of character without a spark of the grace of God. If we put a saint or a good man as the standard, we blind ourselves to ourselves, personal vanity makes us do it; there is no room for personal vanity when the standard is seen to be God Himself.

To cling to my natural virtues is quite sufficient to obscure the work of God in me.

There is a domain of our nature which we as Christians do not cultivate much, viz., the domain of the imagination. Almost the only way we use our imagination is in crossing bridges before we come to them. The religion of Jesus embraces every part of our make-up, the intellectual part, the emotional part, no part must be allowed to atrophy, all must be welded into one by the Holy Spirit.

Learn to distinguish between what isolates you and what insulates you. God insulates; sin isolates, a gloomy, sardonic standing off from everything, the disdain of superiority; only when you are closest to God do you understand that that is its nature.

The natural virtues in some people are charming and delightful, but let a presentation of truth be given they have not seen before, and there is an exhibition of the most extraordinary resentment, proving that all their piety was purely temperamental, an unexplored inheritance from ancestors.

It is an appalling fact that our features tell our moral character unmistakably to those who can read them, and we may be very thankful there are few who can; our safety is in other people's ignorance. In spite of the disguise of refinement, sensuality, selfishness and self-indulgence speak in our features as loud as a thunder-clap. Our inner spirit tells with an indelible mark on every feature, no matter how beautiful or how ugly the features may be. Let us remember that that is how God sees us.

Nothing can hinder God's purpose in a personal life but the person himself.

In this life we must forgo much in order that we might develop a spiritual character which can be a glory to God for Time and Eternity.

In His teaching about discipleship Jesus Christ bases everything on the complete annihilation of individuality and the emancipation of personality. Until this is understood all our talk about discipleship passes into thin air.

When I am baptised with the Holy Ghost my personality is lifted up to its right place, viz., into perfect union with God so that I love Him without hindrance.

Anything that partakes of the nature of swamping my personality out of control is never of God.

NINE

PERSONAL RELATIONSHIP

*T*HE ESSENCE OF Christianity is a personal relationship to Jesus Christ with any amount of room for its outworking.

The appeal of the Gospel is not that it should be preached in order that men might be saved and put right for heaven, but that they might enter into a personal relationship with Jesus Christ here and now.

Discipleship and salvation are two different things: a disciple is one who, realising the meaning of the Atonement, deliberately gives himself up to Jesus Christ in unspeakable gratitude.

The one mark of discipleship is the mastership of Jesus — His right to me from the crown of my head to the sole of my foot.

'If any man would come after Me, let him deny himself,' ie., 'deny his right to himself.' Jesus never swept men off their feet in ecstasy, He always talked on the line that left a man's will in the ascendant until he saw where he was going. It is impossible for a man to give up his right to himself without knowing he is doing it.

Naturally, a man regards his right to himself as the finest thing he has, yet it is the last bridge that prevents Jesus Christ having His way in a life.

The approaches to Jesus are innumerable; the result

of coming to Him can be only one — the dethroning of my right to myself, or I stop short somewhere.

Jesus Christ is always unyielding to my claim to my right to myself.

The one essential element in all our Lord's teaching about discipleship is abandon, no calculation, no trace of self-interest.

Is Jesus Christ absolutely necessary to me? Have I ever shifted the basis of my reasoning on to Incarnate Reason? ever shifted my will on to His will? my right to myself on to His right to me?

What is the personal history between Jesus Christ and myself? Is there anything of the nature of 'the new creation' in me? or is what I call my 'experience' sentimental rubbish placed on top of 'me' as I am?

A disciple is one who not only proclaims God's truth, but one who manifests that he is no longer his own, he has been 'bought with a price.'

Our service is to be a living sacrifice of devotion to Jesus, the secret of which is identity with Him in suffering, in death, and in resurrection (Phil 3:10).

It is possible to be first in suffering for the Truth and in reputation for saintliness, and last in the judgement of the great Searcher of hearts. The whole question is one of heart-relationship to Jesus.

If you remain true to your relationship to Jesus Christ the things that are either right or wrong are never the problem; it is the things that are right but which would impair what He wants you to be that are the problem.

The mark of the saint is the good right things he has the privilege of not doing. There are a hundred and one right and good things which, if you are a disciple of Jesus, you must avoid as you would the devil although there is no devil in them. If our Lord's words

in Matthew 5:29–30 were read more often we would
have a healthier young manhood and womanhood.

Beware of the people who tell you life is simple.
Life is such a mass of complications that no man is
safe apart from God. Coming to Jesus does not sim-
plify life, it simplifies my relationship to God.

The implicit relationship tells more than the
explicit, if you put the explicit first you are apt to
produce sceptics.

When Jesus Christ is 'bringing a son to glory', He
ignores the work he has done; the work has been
allowed as a discipline to perfect his relationship to
the Father.

The work we do for God is made by Him a means
till He has got us to the place where we are willing to
be purified and made of worth to Himself.

Overmuch organisation in Christian work is always
in danger of killing God-born originality; it keeps us
conservative, makes our hands feeble. A false artificial
flow of progress swamps true devotion to Jesus.

Whenever a spiritual movement has been true to
Jesus Christ it has brought forth fruit in a hundred and
one ways the originator of the movement never
dreamed of.

Neither usefulness nor duty is God's ultimate purpose, His aim is to bring out the message of the Gospel, and if that can only be done by His 'bruising' me,
why shouldn't He? We put our intelligent fingers on
God's plan.

God's idea is that individual Christians should
become identified with His purpose for the world.
When Christianity becomes over-organised and
denominational it is incapable of fulfilling our Lord's
commission; it doesn't 'feed His sheep', it can't (Jn
21:15–17).

'I have had visions on the mount'; 'wonderful times

of communion with God' — but is it turning you into an individual infinitely superior to your Lord and Master? one who won't wash feet, but will only give himself up to certain types of meeting?

'If I then, the Lord and the Master, have washed your feet, ye also ought to wash one another's feet': the highest motive is the only motive for the lowliest service. Where do we stand in God's sight under that scrutiny?

A false religion makes me hyper-conscientious — 'I must not do this, or that'; the one lodestar in the religion of Jesus is personal passionate devotion to Him, and oneness with His interests in other lives. Identify yourself with Jesus Christ's interests in others, and life takes on a romantic risk.

Christianity is not service for Jesus Christ, not winning souls, it is nothing less than the life of Jesus being manifested more and more in my mortal flesh.

Beware of allowing the historic Jesus Christ to be taken from you in any shape or form; make it the intensest concern of your spiritual life to accompany the disciples as He went in and out among them in the days of His flesh.

'What has my religion done for me I could not do for myself?' That is a question every man is forced to ask. Religion ostensibly is faith in Someone, or a form of belief in some power, I would be the poorer if I did not have, and I should be able to state in what way I would be poorer.

If my religion is not based on a personal history with Jesus it becomes something I suffer from, not a joyous thing, but something that keeps me from doing what I want to do.

Occasionally we have to revise our ways of looking at God's Providence. The usual way of looking at it is that God presents us with a cup to drink, which is strangely mixed. But there is another aspect which is just as true, perhaps more vitally true, viz., that we present God with a cup to drink, full of a very strange mixture indeed. God will never reverse the cup. He will drink it. Beware of the ingredient of self-will, which ought to have been dissolved by identification with the Death of Jesus, being there when you hand the cup of your life back to God.

TEN

PRAYER

G OD IS NEVER impressed with our earnestness, He promises to answer us when we pray on one ground only, viz., the ground of the Redemption. The Redemption of the Lord Jesus provides me with a place for intercession.

The only way to get into the relationship of 'asking' is to get into the relationship of absolute reliance on the Lord Jesus. 'And this is the confidence that we have in Him....' (1 Jn 5:14–16).

Remember, you have to ask things which are in keeping with the God whom Jesus Christ reveals.

When you pray, what conception have you in your mind — your need, or Jesus Christ's omnipotence? (Jn 14:12–13).

'Asking' in prayer is at once the test of three things — simplicity, stupidity, and certainty of God.

Prayer means that I come in contact with an Almighty Christ, and almighty results happen along the lines He laid down.

It is not that my prayers are so important, that is not the point; God has so made it that by means of intercession certain types of blessing come upon men. In Christian work that is where the 'filling up' comes in; we are apt to bank much more on talking to people.

If I am a Christian, I am not set on saving my own skin, but on seeing that the salvation of God comes through me to others, and the great way is by intercession.

The Bible knows nothing about a gift of prayer, the only prayer the Bible talks about is the prayer that is able to bring down something from God to men.

How impatient we are in dealing with other people! Our actions imply that we think God is asleep, until God brings us to the place where we come on them from above.

The illustrations of prayer our Lord uses are on the line of importunity, a steady, persistent, uninterrupted habit of prayer.

God puts us in circumstances where He can answer the prayer of His Son (Jn 17), and the prayer of the Holy Ghost (Rom 8:26).

The reason for intercession is not that God *answers* prayer, but that God tells us to pray.

God never answers prayer to prove His own might.

The answers to prayer never come by introspection but always as a surprise. We don't hear God because we are so full of noisy introspective requests.

Spiritual certainty in prayer is God's certainty, not a side-eddy of sanctimoniousness.

Prayer is the vital breath of the Christian; not the thing that makes him alive, but the evidence that he *is* alive.

The very powers of darkness are paralysed by prayer. No wonder Satan tries to keep our minds fussy in active work till we cannot think to pray.

God is not meant to answer *our* prayers, He is answering the prayer of Jesus Christ in our lives; by our prayers we come to discern what God's mind is, and that is declared in John 17.

According to the New Testament, prayer is God's answer to our poverty, not a power we exercise to obtain an answer.

Intercession does not develop the one who intercedes, it blesses the lives of those for whom he intercedes. The reason so few of us intercede is because we don't understand this.

By intercessory prayer we can hold off Satan from other lives and give the Holy Ghost a chance with them. No wonder Jesus put such tremendous emphasis on prayer!

If your crowd knows you as a man or woman of prayer, they have a right to expect from you a nobler type of conduct than from others.

If I pray that someone else may be, or do, something which I am not, and don't intend to do, my praying is paralysed.

When you put God first you will get your times of prayer easily because God can entrust them to the soul who won't use them in an irrational way and give an occasion to the enemy to enter in.

Watch God's ways in your life, you will find He is developing you as He does the trees and the flowers, a deep silent working of the God of Creation.

The enemy goes all he can against our communion with God, against our solitude with God, he tries to prevent us from 'drawing our breath in the fear of the Lord.'

The greatest answer to prayer is that I am brought into a perfect understanding with God, and that alters my view of actual things.

We must steadfastly work out repentance in intercessory prayer.

Beware lest activity in proclaiming the Truth should mean a cunning avoidance of spiritual concentration in intercession.

The lost sight of God inevitably follows spiritual teaching that has not a corresponding balance of private prayer.

See that you do not use the trick of prayer to cover up what you know you ought to do.

The meaning of prayer is that I bring power to bear upon another soul that is weak enough to yield and strong enough to resist; hence the need for strenuous intercessory prayer.

Never try to make people agree with your point of view, begin the ministry of intercession. The only Being worth agreeing with is the Lord Jesus Christ. Remember 1 John 5:16.

The prayer of the saints is never self-important, but always God-important.

What happens when a saint prays is that the Paraclete's almighty power is brought to bear on the one for whom he is praying.

God does not give faith in answer to prayer: He reveals Himself in answer to prayer, and faith is exercised spontaneously.

ELEVEN

PREACHING

A PERSONAL TESTIMONY feeds you from hand to mouth; you must have more equipment than that if you are to preach the Gospel.

The preacher must be part of his message, he must be incorporated in it. That is what the baptism of the Holy Ghost did for the disciples. When the Holy Ghost came at Pentecost He made these men living epistles of the teaching of Jesus, not human gramophones recording the facts of His life.

If you stand true as a disciple of Jesus He will make your preaching the kind of message that is incarnate as well as oral.

To preach the Gospel makes *you* a sacrament; but if the Word of God has not become incorporated into you, your preaching is 'a clanging cymbal', it has never cost you anything, never taken you through repentance and heart-break.

We have not to explain how a man comes to God, instead of bringing men to God, that hinders; an explanation of the Atonement never drew anyone to God, the exalting of Jesus Christ, and Him crucified, does draw men to God (see John 12:32).

Remember, you go among men as a representative of Jesus Christ.

The preacher's duty is not to convict men of sin, or to make them realise how bad they are, but to bring them into contact with God until it is easy for them to believe in Him.

No man is ever the same after listening to the truth, he may say he pays no attention to it, he may appear to forget all about it, but at any moment the truth may spring up into his consciousness and destroy all his peace of mind.

The great snare in Christian work is this — 'Do remember the people you are talking to.' We have to remain true to God and His message, not to a knowledge of the people, and as we rely on the Holy Spirit we will find God works His marvels in His own way.

Live in the reality of the Truth while you preach it.

Most of us prefer to live in a particular phase of the Truth, and that is where we get intolerant and pig-headed, religiously determined that everyone who does not agree with us must be wrong. We preach in the Name of God what He won't own.

God's denunciation will fall on us if in our preaching we tell people they must be holy and we ourselves are not holy. If we are not working out in our private life the messages we are handing out, we will deepen the condemnation of our own souls as messengers of God.

Our message acts like a boomerang; it is dangerous if it does not.

A good clear emotional expression contains within it the peril of satisfactory expression while the life is miles away from the preaching. The life of a preacher speaks louder than his words.

There is no use condemning sensuality or wordly-mindedness and compromise in other people if there is the slightest inclination for these in our own soul.

It is all very well to preach, the easiest thing in the world to give people a vision of what God wants; it is another matter to come into the sordid conditions of ordinary life and make the vision real there.

Beware of hypocrisy with God, especially if you are in no danger of hypocrisy among men.

Penetration attracts hearers to God; ingenuity attracts to the preacher. Dexterity is always an indication of shallowness.

A clever exposition is never right because the Spirit of God is not clever. Beware of cleverness, it is the great cause of hypocrisy in a preacher.

Don't be impatient with yourself, because the longer you are in satisfying yourself with an expression of the Truth the better will you satisfy God.

Impressive preaching is rarely Gospel-preaching: Gospel-preaching is based on the great mystery of belief in the Atonement, which belief is created in others, not by my impressiveness, but by the insistent conviction of the Holy Spirit.

There is far more wrought by the Word of God than we will ever understand, and if I substitute anything for it, fine thinking, eloquent speech, the devil's victory is enormous, but I am of no more use than a puff of wind.

The determination to be a fool if necessary is the golden rule for a preacher.

We have to preach something which to the wisdom of this world is foolishness. If the wisdom of this world is right, then God is foolish; if God is wise, the wisdom of this world is foolishness (see 1 Corinthians 1:18–25). Where we go wrong is when we apologise for God.

If you are standing for the truth of God you are sure to experience reproach, and if you open your mouth to vindicate yourself you will lose what you were on the point of gaining. Let the ignominy and the shame come, be 'weak in Him'.

Never assume anything that has not been made yours by faith and the experience of life; it is presumptuous to do so. On the other hand, be ready to pay the price of 'foolishness' in proclaiming to others what is really yours.

People only want the kind of preaching which does not declare the demands of a holy God. 'Tell us that God is loving, not that He is holy, and that He demands we should be holy.' The problem is not with the gross sinners, but with the intellectual, cultured, religious-to-the-last-degree people.

All the winsome preaching of the Gospel is an insult to the Cross of Christ. What is needed is the probe of the Spirit of God straight down to a man's conscience till his whole nature shouts at him, 'That is right, and *you* are wrong.'

It is the preacher's contact with reality that enables the Holy Spirit to strip off the sophistries of those who listen, and when He does that, you find it is the best people who go down first under conviction.

A great psychological law too little known is that the line of appeal is conditioned by the line of attraction. If I seek to attract men, that will be the line on which my aggressive work will have to be done.

To whom is our appeal? To none but those God sends you to. You can't get men to come; nobody could get you to come until you came. 'The wind bloweth where it listeth,...so is everyone that is born of the Spirit.'

Many of the theological terms used nowadays have no grip, we talk glibly about sin, and about salvation; but let the truth be presented along the line of a man's deep personal need, and at once it is arresting.

Some of us are rushing on at such a headlong pace in Christian work, wanting to vindicate God in a great

Revival, but if God gave a revival we would be the first to forget Him and swing off on some false fire.

'...not slothful in business,' ie., the Lord's business. Don't exhaust yourself with other things.

Beware as of the devil of good taste being your standard in presenting the truth of God.

'Wherefore henceforth know we no man after the flesh' (2 Cor 5:16); that is the way we do know men — according to our common-sense estimates. The man who knows God has no right to estimate other men according to his common-sense judgement, he has to bring in revelation facts which will make him a great deal more lenient in his judgement. To have a little bit only of God's point of view makes us immensely bitter in our judgement.

Beware lest your reserve in public has the effect of God Almighty's decree to the sea — 'Hitherto shalt thou come, but no further.' I have no business in God's service if I have any personal reserve, I am to be broken bread and poured-out wine in His hands.

If you are living a life of reckless trust in God the impression given to your congregation is that of the reserve power of God, while personal reserve leaves the impression that you are condescending to them.

We should give instruction unconsciously; if you give instruction consciously in a dictatorial mood, you simply flatter your own spiritual conceit.

Have you never met the person whose religious life is so exact that you are terrified at coming near him? Never have an exercise of religion that blots God clean out.

Remember two things: be natural yourself, and let God be naturally Himself through you. Very few of us have got to the place of being worthily natural, any number of us are un-worthily natural, that is, we reveal the fact that we have never taken the trouble to discipline ourselves.

Don't be discouraged if you suffer from physical aphasia, the only cure for it is to go ahead, remembering that nervousness overcome is power.

Beware of being disappointed with yourself in delivery; ignore the record of your nerves.

Learn to be vicarious in public prayer. Allow two rivers to come through you: the river of God, and the river of human interests. Beware of the danger of preaching in prayer, of being doctrinal.

When you preach, you speak for God, and from God to the people; in prayer, you talk to God for the people, and your proper place is among the people as one of them. It is to be a vicarious relation, not the flinging of theology at their heads from the pulpit.

Always come from God to men; never be so impertinent as to come from the presence of anyone else.

How do interruptions affect you? If you allot your day and say, 'I am going to give so much time to this, and so much to that,' and God's Providence upsets your time-table, what becomes of your spirituality? Why, it flies out of the window! it is not based on God, there is nothing spiritual about it, it is purely mechanical. The great secret is to learn how to draw on God all the time.

Whenever you are discovered as being exhausted, take a good humiliating dose of John 21:15–17. The whole secret of shepherding is that someone else reaches the Saviour through your heart as a pathway.

Beware of making God's truth simpler than He has made it Himself.

By the preaching of the Gospel God creates what was never there before, viz., faith in Himself on the ground of the Redemption.

People say, 'Do preach the simple Gospel,' if they

mean by 'the simple Gospel' the thing we have always heard, the thing that keeps us sound asleep, then the sooner God sends a thrust through our stagnant minds the better.

If any man's preaching does not make me brace myself up and watch my feet and my ways, one of two things is the reason — either the preacher is unreal, or I hate being better.

A joyous, humble belief in your message will compel attention.

Sermons may weary, the Gospel never does.

TWELVE

PREPARATION

*I*T IS BY thinking with your pen in hand that you will get to the heart of your subject.

'The heart of the righteous studieth to answer' (Prov 15:28). To give your congregation extemporaneous thinking, ie., thinking without study, is an insult — ponderous 'nothings'. The preacher should give his congregation the result of strenuous thinking in un-studied, extemporaneous speech.

Extemporaneous speech is not extemporaneous thinking, but speech that has been so studied that you are possessed unconsciously with what you are saying.

Never get a studied form; prepare yourself mentally, morally, and spiritually, and you need never fear.

The great thing is not to hunt for texts, but to live in the big comprehensive truths of the Bible and texts will hunt you.

To talk about 'getting a message', is a mistake. It is preparation of myself that is required more than of my message.

Don't go to your Bible in a yawning mood.

As a student of the Word of God, keep your mind and heart busy with the great truths concerning God, the Lord Jesus Christ, the Holy Spirit, the Atonement, sin, suffering, etc.

Slay on the threshold of your mind the thing that makes you sit down mentally and say, *'I can't.'* Why be saved and sanctified in a rusty indolent case?

In impromptu speaking, begin naturally, and the secret of beginning naturally is to forget you are religious. Many wear a crushing religious garb.

Beware of detaching yourself from your theme in order to heed the way you present it. Never be afraid of expressing what is really *you.*

To develop your expression in public you must do a vast amount of writing in private. Write out your problems before God. Go direct to Him about everything.

Time spent on the great fundamental revelations given by the Holy Spirit is apt to be looked upon as a waste of time — 'We must get to practical work.'

The work we do in preparation is meant to get our minds into such order that they are at the service of God for His inspiration.

Conscious inspiration is mercifully rare or we would make inspiration our god.

Don't chisel your subject too much. Trust the reality of your nature and the reality of your subject.

The discipline of your own powers is a very precious acquirement in the service of God; it delivers you from breathless uncertainty and possible hysterics. Learn to respect the findings of your own mind.

Always check private delight in preparation. Close your preparation with prayer and leave it with God till wanted.

When you speak, abandon yourself in confidence; don't try to recall fine points in preparation.

The burning heart while Jesus talks with us and opens up the Scriptures to us is a blessed experience, but the burning heart will die down to ashes unless we keep perennially right with God.

Spiritual insight is in accordance with the development of heart-purity.

Every domain of our life which comes under the apprehension of the Spirit of God is a call to cultivate that particular domain for Him. The trouble is that we won't break up the new soil of our lives for God.

Spiritual sloth must be the greatest grief to the Holy Ghost. Sloth has always a moral reason, not a physical one; the self-indulgent nature must be slothful.

Learn to fast over your subject in private; do the mechanical work and trust God for the inspirational in delivery.

Don't memorise what you have to say or you will serve up *'cauld kale het!'*

In order to expound a passage, live in it well beforehand.

Keep yourself full with reading. Reading gives you a vocabulary.

Don't read to remember; read to realise.

The speaker without notes must have two things entirely at his command — the Bible and his mother-tongue.

An impromptu speaking, never try to recall, always plunge.

Let the centre of your subject grip you, then you will express its heart unconsciously.

Get moved by your message, and it will move others in a corresponding way.

Watch how God by His angels elbows you out of the hour you thought you were going to get with your Bible — only you will never call them 'angels' unless you are filled with the Holy Spirit. 'That objectionable person' was really an angel of God to you, saying, 'Get this thing worked out.'

THIRTEEN

REDEMPTION

GOD DOES NOT ask us to be good men and women: He asks us to understand that we are not good; to believe that 'none is good save one, even God,' and that the grace of God was manifested in the Redemption that it might cover the incompleteness of man.

When a man experiences salvation it is not his belief that saves him; teaching goes wrong when it puts a man's belief as the ground of his salvation. Salvation is God's 'bit' entirely.

The danger is to preach a subjective theology, something that wells up on the inside. The Gospel of the New Testament is based on the absoluteness of the Redemption.

The great thing about the Redemption is that it deals with *sin*, ie., my claim to my right to myself, not primarily with man's sins. It is one of the most flattering things to go and rescue the degraded, one of the social passions of mankind, but not necessarily the most Christian: it is quite another thing to tell men who are among the best of men that what Jesus Christ asks of them is that they give up the right to themselves to Him.

The great thing about the Gospel is that it should be preached. Never get distressed over not seeing immediate results. No prophet of the Old Testament, or apostle of the New (or saint of the present day), ever fully understood the import of what he said or did, hence to work for immediate results is to make myself a director of the Holy Ghost.

God is no respecter of persons with regard to salvation, but He has a tremendous respect for Christian character. There are degrees in glory which are determined by our obedience.

Salvation is a free gift through the Redemption; positions in the Kingdom are not gifts, but attainments.

There is a difference between salvation and saintliness, between being redeemed and proving myself a redeemed man. I may live a life of sordid self-seeking on the basis of the Redemption, or I may live a life which 'manifests the life of the Lord Jesus in my mortal flesh.'

Jesus Christ did not send out the disciples to save souls, but to 'make disciples', men and women who manifest a life in accordance with the life of their Redeemer.

A charge made against some methods of evangelism is that self-interest is made the basis of the whole thing: salvation is looked upon as a kind of insurance scheme whereby I am delivered from punishment and put right for heaven. But let a man experience *deliverance from sin*, and his rejoicing is not in his own interests, but that he is thereby enabled to be of use to God and his fellow men.

The bedrock permanent thing about Christianity is the forgiveness of God, not sanctification and personal holiness — the great abiding thing underneath is infinitely more rugged than that; it is all the New Testament means by that terrific word *'forgiveness'*. 'In whom we have our redemption through His blood, the forgiveness of sins' (Eph 1:7).

The virtue of our Redemption comes to us through the obedience of the Son of God — 'though He were a Son, yet learned He obedience by the things which He suffered...' (Heb 5:8–9). Our view of obedience has become so distorted through sin that we cannot understand how it could be said of Jesus that He 'learned' obedience; He was the only One of whom it could be said, because He was 'without sin'. He did not learn obedience in order *to be* a Son: He came *as* Son to redeem mankind.

Our Lord came to make atonement for the sin of the world, not by any impulse of a noble nature, but by the perfect conscious Self-sacrifice whereby alone God could redeem man.

Beware of the craze for unity. It is God's will that all Christians should be one with Him as Jesus Christ is one with Him (Jn 17:22), but that is a very different thing from the tendency abroad to-day towards a unity on a basis that ignores the Atonement.

Until we have become spiritual by new birth the Atonement of Jesus has no meaning for us; it only begins to get meaning when we live 'in heavenly places in Christ Jesus'.

Salvation is based on the *revelation* fact that God has redeemed the world from the possibility of condemnation on account of sin (Rom 5:12, 20–1): the *experience* of salvation means that a man can be regenerated, can have the disposition of the Son of God put into him, viz., the Holy Spirit.

Belief in the Redemption is difficult because it needs self-surrender first.

Do I believe that everything that has been touched by the consequences of man's sin is going to be put absolutely right by God through the Redemption?

Redemption is the Reality which alters inability into ability.

The mighty Redemption of God is made actual in my experience by the living efficacy of the Holy Ghost.

FOURTEEN

SANCTIFICATION

*B*EWARE OF PREACHING Sanctification without knowing Jesus; we are saved and sanctified in order that we might know Him.

'But of Him are ye in Christ Jesus who of God is made unto us wisdom, and righteousness, and sanctification, and redemption' (1 Cor 1:30). Jesus Christ *is* all these, they are not things He works out apart from Himself.

We cannot earn things from God, we can only take what is given us. Salvation, sanctification, eternal life, are all gifts wrought out in us through the Atonement. The question is, am I working out what God works in?

It is quite true to say 'I can't live a holy life'; but you can decide to let Jesus make you holy. 'I can't do away with my past'; but you can decide to let Jesus do away with it. That is the issue to push.

We use the word 'consecration' before sanctification, it should be used after sanctification. The fundamental meaning of consecration is the separating of a holy thing to God, not the separating of an un-holy thing to be made holy.

'...present your bodies a living sacrifice, holy, acceptable unto God,' says the apostle Paul. You cannot separate to God what God has not purified.

If I make personal holiness a cause instead of an effect I become shallow, no matter how profound I seem. It means I am far more concerned about being speckless than about being real; far more concerned about keeping my garments white than about being devoted to Jesus Christ.

The idea that I grow holy as I go on is foreign to the New Testament. There must have been a place where I was identified with the death of Jesus: 'I have been crucified with Christ...;' That is the meaning of sanctification. Then I grow *in* holiness.

Jesus Christ can make my disposition as pure as His own. That is the claim of the Gospel.

The saints have gone to sleep, 'Thank God, I am saved and sanctified, it is all right now': you are simply in the right place to maintain the life which is going to confront the world and never be subdued by the world.

'Now I am sanctified the world has no attraction for me.' But remember, the world is what the Holy Spirit sees, not what you see. It is not gross sins that are the attraction, but things that are part of God's creation, things 'in the land of Canaan', they creep in gradually and you begin to think according to pagan standards and only in a crisis realise you have not been standing with God.

God has staked His reputation on the work of Jesus Christ in the souls of the men and women whom He has saved and sanctified.

If we are to be of any use to God in facing present-day problems we must be prepared to run the sanctification-metaphysic for all it is worth.

The great fever in people's blood to-day is, 'Do something'; 'Be practical'. The great need is for the one who is un-practical enough to get down to the heart of the matter, viz., personal sanctification. Practical work not based on an understanding of what sanctification means is simply beating the air.

The test of sanctification is not our talk about holiness and singing pious hymns; but, what are we like where no one sees us? with those who know us best?

It is perilously possible to credit God with all our mean little prejudices even after we are sanctified.

Pious talk paralyses the power to live piously, the energy of the life goes into the talk — sanctimonious instead of sanctified. Unless your mind is free from jealousy, envy, spite, your pious words only increase your hypocrisy.

Beware of sentimentality; it means something has been aroused in me that I don't intend to work out.

Wherever there is true teaching of the Gospel there will be both salvation and sanctification taking place.

If you are called to preach, God will put you through 'mills' that are not meant for you personally, He is making you suitable bread to nourish other lives. It is after sanctification you are put through these things.

If I exalt Sanctification, I preach people into despair; but if I lift up Jesus Christ, people learn the way to be made holy. 'For I determined not to know anything among you, save Jesus Christ, and Him crucified' (1 Cor 2:2).

It is a great snare to think that when you are sanctified you cannot make mistakes; you can make mistakes so irreparably terrible that the only safeguard is to 'walk in the light, as God is in the light.'

When you come under the searchlight of God after sanctification, you realise much more keenly what sin is than ever you could have done before.

The deliverances of God are not what the saint delights in, but in the fact that *God* delivered him; not in the fact that he is sanctified, but that *God* sanctified him; the whole attention of the mind is on God.

We are saved and sanctified not for service, but to

be absolutely Jesus Christ's, the consuming passion of the life is for Him.

Never try to build sanctification on an unconfessed sin, on a duty left undone; confess the wrong, do what you ought to have done, then God will clear away all the hyper-conscientious rubbish.

In sanctification it has to be a valediction once and for ever to confidence in everyone and everything but God.

You can always test the worth of your sanctification. If there is the slightest trace of self-conscious superiority about it, it has never touched the fringe of the garment of Christ.

'I lay down My life,' said Jesus; *'I lay it down of Myself.'* If you are sanctified, you will do the same. It has nothing to do with 'Deeper Death to Self', it has to do with the glorious fact that I have a self, a personality, that I can sacrifice with glad alacrity to Jesus every day I live.

FIFTEEN

SIN

S IN IS NOT a man's problem, it is God's.

Beware of attempting to diagnose sin unless you have the inner pang that you are one of the worst of sinners.

Whenever you talk about sin, it must be 'my' sin. So long as you speak of 'sins' you evade Jesus Christ for yourself.

Sin is the outcome of a relationship God never ordained, a relationship which maintains itself by means of a wrong disposition, viz., my claim to my right to myself. That is the essence of sin.

My right to myself is not merely something I claim, but something that continually makes me insist on my own way.

Whenever God touches sin it is independence that is touched and that awakens resentment in the human heart. Independence must be blasted clean out, there must be no such thing left, only freedom, which is very different. Freedom is the ability not to insist on my rights, but to see that God gets His.

There are people whose actual lives shock us and there are those whose actual lives are speckless, but whose ruling disposition is 'my claim to my right to myself'. Watch Jesus Christ with them both, and you get the attitude we have lost.

Jesus Christ never faced men as we do; you may put

before Him 'publicans and sinners' and clean-living, moral men, and you find He is much sterner with the latter. To recognise this would mean a revolution in our outlook.

Original sin is 'doing without God'. That phrase covers sin in its beginning in human consciousness and its final analysis in the sight of God.

'For from within, out of the heart of man proceed...' (Mk 7:21–3). We should get into the habit of estimating ourselves by the rugged statements of our Lord.

The thing that makes me feel I am different from 'the common herd' never came from God: I am not different. Remember, the same stuff that makes the criminal makes the saint.

A saint is 'a new creation', made by the Last Adam out of the progeny of the first Adam no matter how degraded.

'...Christ Jesus came into the world to save sinners' (1 Tim 1:15). What is a sinner? Everyone who is not one with Jesus as He is one with God.

Our Lord did not scathe sin; He came to save from it.

We are apt to put the superb blessings of the Gospel as something for a special few, they are for sinners saved by grace.

A man may be magnificently saved and appallingly backward in development, or he may be a maturely developed saint, like the apostle Paul; but neither is more than saved by God's grace.

When Jesus Christ begins to get His way He is merciless with the thing that is not of God.

As long as things are kept covered up we think God's judgement is severe, but let the Holy Ghost reveal the secret vileness of sin till it blazes out in a conspicuous glare, and we realise that His judgement is right.

The reason men enclose themselves away from the Gospel is that conviction of sin upsets the inner balance of mind, consequently of bodily health, but when once a man is convinced that holiness is of more importance than bodily health, he lets all go to get holy.

The first appeal of present-day evangelism is apt to be, not on the line of how to get rid of sin, but how to be put right for heaven, consequently men are not convicted of sin, but left with a feeling of something insufficient in life.

The only hope for a man lies not in giving him an example of how to behave, but in the preaching of Jesus Christ as the Saviour from *sin*. The heart of every man gets hope when he hears that.

Our Lord never sympathised with sin; He came to 'proclaim liberty to the captives,' a very different thing. We have to see that we don't preach a theology of sympathy, but the theology of a Saviour from sin.

It is not our business to convict men of sin, the Holy Ghost alone convicts of sin, our duty is to lift up the One who sets free from sin. It is not a question of something being curbed, or counteracted, or sat on, it is a radical alteration on the inside, then I have to assimilate that alteration so that it is manifested in the practical relationships of my life.

The life of the Holy Spirit in a saint is fierce and violent against any tendency to sin.

The attitude of Jesus towards *sin* is to be our attitude towards *sins*.

When conviction of sin by the Holy Spirit comes it gives us an understanding of the deeps of our personality we are otherwise not conscious of (Jn 16:8–11).

The forgiveness of God penetrates to the very heart

of His nature and to the very heart of man's nature. That is why God cannot forgive until a man realises what sin is.

Sin is reality; sins are actuality.

Measure your growth in grace by your sensitiveness to sin.

Many a man gets to the place where he will call himself a sinner, but he does not so readily come to the place where he says, 'Against Thee, Thee only, have I sinned...'

Salvation from sin is frequently confounded with deliverance from sins. A man can deliver himself from sins without any special work of God's grace. The bedrock of New Testament salvation is repentance, and repentance is based on relationship to a Person.

A great many people are delighted to hear about the life of Jesus, its holiness and sublimity, but when the Holy Ghost begins to convict them of sin, they resent it, and resent it deeply.

Conviction of sin in the beginning is child's play compared with the conviction the Holy Ghost brings to a mature saint (see 1 Timothy 1:15).

Humiliation by conviction of sin is rare to-day. You can never be humiliated by another human being after the conviction of sin the Holy Ghost gives.

On the threshold of the Christian life people talk a lot about sin, but there is no realisation of what sin is, all that is seen is the effects of sin.

If we are ever going to come anywhere near understanding what our Lord's agony in the Garden of Gethsemane represents, we have to get beyond the small ideas of our particular religious experiences and be brought to see sin as God sees it — 'For He hath made *Him to be sin* for us, *who knew no sin;* that we might be made the righteousness of God in Him.'

If we eliminate the supernatural purpose of Jesus Christ's coming, viz., to deliver us from sin, we become traitors to God's revelation.

The Cross of Christ is God's last and endless Word. There the prince of this world is judged, there sin is killed, and pride is done to death, there lust is frozen, and self-interest slaughtered, not one can get through.

It was not social crimes, but the great primal sin of independence of God, that brought the Son of God to Calvary.

SIXTEEN

STUDY

STUDY TO BEGIN with can never be easy; the determination to form systematic mental habits is the only secret. Don't begin anything with reluctance.

Beware of any cleverness that keeps you from working. No one is born a worker; men are born poets and artists, but we have to make ourselves 'labourers'.

The discipline of our mind is the one domain God has put in our keeping. It is impossible to be of any use to God if we are lazy. God won't cure laziness, we have to cure it.

More danger arises from physical laziness (which is called 'brain fag') than from almost any other thing.

Inspiration won't come irrespective of study, but only because of it. Don't trust to inspiration, use your own 'axe' (Ps 74:5). Work! Think! Don't luxuriate on the mount!

The demand for inspiration is the measure of our laziness. Do the things that don't come by inspiration.

It is difficult to get yourself under control to do work you are not used to, the time spent seems wasted at first, but get at it again. The thing that hinders control is impulse.

Your mind can never be under your control unless you bring it there; there is no gift for control. You may pray till Doomsday but your brain will never concentrate if you don't make it concentrate.

In the most superficial matters put yourself under control, your own control. Be as scrupulously punctual in your private habits as you would be in a Government office.

Don't insult God by telling Him He forgot to give you any brains when you were born. We all have brains, what we need is *work*.

It is better for your mental life to study several subjects at once rather than one alone. What exhausts the brain is not *using* it, but abusing it by nervous waste in other directions. As a general rule, the brain can never do too much.

You can never work by impulse, you can only work by steady patient plod. It is the odd five minutes that tells.

To learn a thing is different from thinking out a problem. The only way to learn a thing is to keep at it uninterruptedly, day after day, whether you feel like it or not, and you will wake up one morning and find the thing is learned.

Beware of succumbing to failure as inevitable; make it the stepping-stone to success.

In beginning to study a new subject you do it by repeated starts until you get your mind into a certain channel, after that the subject becomes full of sustained interest.

Beware of mental lounging. Whenever we see notebooks for study, or work of any kind waiting to be done, we either go into dreamland, or we gather everything around us in an enormously bustling style, but we never do good solid work. It is nothing in the world but a habit of nerves which we have to check, and take time to see that we do.

A subject has never truly gripped you until you are mentally out of breath with it.

We have no business to go on impulses spiritually, we have to form 'the mind which was also in Christ Jesus'. People say their impulses are their guide — 'I feel impelled to do this, or that' — that may be sufficient indication that they should not do it.

Remember, there must always be a mechanical outlet for spiritual inspiration.

We infect our surroundings with our own personal character. If I make my study a place of stern industry, it will act as an inspiration every time I go into it; but if I am lazy there, the place will revenge itself on me.

Note two things about your intelligence: first, when your intelligence feels numb, quit at once, and play or sleep; for the time being the brain must recuperate; second, when you feel a fidget of associated ideas, take yourself sternly in hand and say, 'You shall study, so it's no use whining.'

Mental stodge is different. Mental stodge is the result of one of three forms of over-feeding — too much dinner, too much reading, or too much meetings.

Irritation may be simply the result of not using your brain. Remember, the brain gets exhausted when it is not doing anything.

Beware of saying, 'I haven't time to read the Bible, or to pray'; say rather, 'I haven't disciplined myself to do these things.'

Before any habit is formed you must put yourself under mechanical laws of obedience, and the higher the emotion started by the Spirit of God, the keener must be the determination to commit yourself.

If we have no system of work we shall easily come to think we are working when we are only thinking of working, that we are busy when we are only engaged.

The more we talk about work, the less we work, and the same with prayer.

We must be willing to do in the spiritual domain what we have to do in the natural domain if we want to develop, viz., discipline ourselves.

Vision is an inspiration to stand us in good stead in the drudgery of discipline; the temptation is to despise the discipline.

Enchain your body to habitual obedience.

Beware of being haunted by a suppressed dissatisfaction with the arrangements of your actual life — *get* the right programme! The secret of slacking is just here.

SEVENTEEN

THE TEACHING OF JESUS

*O*UR LORD DID not come to this earth to *teach* men to be holy: He came to *make* men holy, and His teaching is applicable only on the basis of experimental Redemption.

The teaching of Jesus is not first; what *is* first is that He came to give us a totally new heredity, and the Sermon on the Mount describes the way that heredity will work out.

A good way to find out how much stodge there is in our spiritual life is to read the Sermon on the Mount and see how obtuse we are to the greater part of what Jesus Christ taught.

There is a calm deliberation about the injunctions in the Sermon on the Mount; we are not asked to obey them until the Holy Spirit brings them to our remembrance, when He does, the question is, will I exercise the disposition given me in regeneration and react in my actual life in accordance with the Mind of Christ?

Weighing the *pros and cons* for and against a statement of Jesus Christ's means that for the time being I refuse to obey Him.

We are never justified in taking any line of action other than that indicated by the teaching of Jesus and made possible for us by the grace of God.

Our Lord's teaching does not mean anything to a man until it does, and then it means everything.

Make your mind sure of what our Lord taught, and then insist and re-insist on it to the best of your ability.

Distortions of belief come because principles are put in the place of Jesus Christ. I must have a personal relationship to Him first, and then let the Holy Spirit apply His teaching.

Nothing must switch the disciple's loyalty to his Lord by loyalty to principles deduced from His teaching.

There are no infallible principles, only an infallible Person.

All my devotion is an insult to God unless every bit of my practical life squares with Jesus Christ's demands.

Beware of being negligent in some lesser thing while being good in some spiritual thing, eg., you may be good in a prayer meeting while not good in the matter of cleaning your boots. It is a real peril, and springs from selecting some one thing our Lord taught as our standard instead of God Himself.

Matthew 5:48 is the standard for the Christian: 'Ye therefore shall be perfect, as your heavenly Father is perfect.' Size yourself up with a good sense of humour — '*me*, perfect!' That is what Jesus Christ has undertaken to do.

The religion of Jesus is morality transfigured by spirituality; we have to be moral right down to the depths of our motives.

It cannot be too often emphasised that our Lord never asks us to do other than all that good upright men do, but He does ask that we do just those same things from an entirely different motive (Mt 5:20).

We should make less excuses for the weaknesses of

a Christian than for any other man. A Christian has God's honour at stake.

When a man is regenerated and bears the Name of Christ the Spirit of God will see to it that he is scrutinised by the world, and the more we are able to meet that scrutiny the healthier will we be as Christians.

Civilised organisations were never more deadly opposed to the teaching of Jesus than in the present age.

Whenever an organisation begins to be conscious of itself, its spiritual power goes because it is living for its own propaganda. Movements which were started by the Spirit of God have crystallised into something God has had to blight because the golden rule for spiritual work has been departed from (see John 12:24).

'I am not come to destroy, but to fulfil' (Mt 5:17). Our Lord was not *anti* anything; He put into existing institutions a ruling principle which if obeyed would reconstruct them.

If you have never been brought close enough to Jesus to realise that He teaches things that grossly offend you as a natural man, I question whether you have ever seen Him.

Immediately you get out of touch with God, you are in a hell of chaos. That is always in the background of the teaching of Jesus (cf. Mt 5:21–6). That is why the teaching of Jesus produces such consternation in the natural man.

Whenever a truth comes home to me my first reaction is to fling it back on you, but the Spirit of God brings it straight home, 'Thou art the man.' We always want to lash others when we are sick with our own disobedience.

The scrutiny we give other people should be for ourselves. You will never be able to cast out the mote

in your brother's eye unless you have had a beam
removed, or to be removed, from your own eye (Mt
7:3–4).

It is perilously possible to do one of two things —
bind burdens on people you have no intention of
helping them lift, or placidly to explain away the full
purport of our Lord's teaching (see Luke 11:46).

Divorced from supernatural new birth the teaching
of Jesus has no application to me, it only results in
despair.

Our Lord's teaching about the maimed life and the
mature life has not been sufficiently recognised. You
can never be mature unless you have been fanatical
(see Matthew 5:29–30, 48).

'Whosoever shall compel thee to go one mile, go
with him twain' (Mt 5:41). If you are a saint the Lord
will tax your walking capacity to the limit.

It is a slow business teaching a community living
below the Christian level, I have to act according to
the Christian ethic while not ignoring the fact that I
am dealing with a community which lives away
below it. The fact that I live with a degenerate crowd
does not alter my duty, I have to behave as a disciple
of Jesus.

EIGHTEEN

TEMPTATION

*T*O BE RAISED above temptation belongs to God only.

Wherever there is moral responsibility there is temptation, ie., the testing of what a man holds in his own person.

The old Puritan idea that the devil tempts men had this remarkable effect, it produced the man of iron who fought; the modern idea of blaming his heredity or his circumstances produces the man who succumbs at once.

When we say a thing is 'Satanic' we mean something abominable according to our standards: the Bible means something remarkably subtle and wise. Satanic temptations are not bestial, those temptations have to do with a man's own stupidity and wrongdoing.

The Holy Ghost is the only One who can detect the temptations of Satan, neither our common sense nor our human wisdom can detect them as temptations.

Every temptation of Satan is the acme of human wisdom, but immediately the Spirit of God is at work in a man the hollow mockery at its heart is recognised.

Jesus Christ deals with Satan as the manifestation of something for which man is held responsible. Man is nowhere held responsible for the devil.

The temptation in Christian work to-day is to turn

our sympathy towards human beings, 'Put man's needs first.' No, sympathy with God first, let Him work as He will.

If you allow human sympathy to make you susceptible to the Satanic side of things, you instantly sever yourself from the susceptibility which in all temptation ought to be turned God-wards.

Our Lord's words to Peter, 'But He turned and said unto Peter, Get thee behind Me, Satan: for thou art an offence unto Me: for thou savourest not the things that be of God, but those that be of man' (Mt 16:23) crystallise for us His authoritative view of the conclusions of man's mind, when that mind has not been formed by the Holy Spirit, viz., that it is densely and satanically incapable of understanding His form of thought.

Satan does not tempt to gross sins, the one thing he tempts to is putting myself as master instead of God.

Beware of removing our Lord into a religious wardrobe where the cast-off haloes of the saints are kept, but remember that 'we have not a high priest that cannot be touched with the feeling of our infirmities; but one that hath been in all points tempted like as we are, yet without sin' (Heb 4:15; cf Heb 2:11).

How are we to face the tempter? By prayer? No. With the Word of God? No. Face the tempter with Jesus Christ, and He will apply the word of God to you, and the temptation will cease. 'For in that He Himself hath suffered being tempted, He is able to succour them that are tempted' (Heb 2:18).

The moments of severest temptation are the moments of His divinest succour.

NINETEEN

TESTIMONY

*I*T IS NEVER our testimony that keeps our experience right: our experience makes us testify.

To testify is part of the life of every Christian, but because you have a personal testimony it does not follow that you are called to preach.

To say what God has done for you is testimony, but you have to preach more than you have experienced — more than anyone has ever experienced; you have to preach Jesus Christ. Present the Object of your faith, the Lord Jesus, lift Him up, and then either give your testimony, or know you have one to give.

To say a thing is the sure way to begin to believe it. That is why it is so necessary to testify to what Jesus Christ has done for you.

The false mood creeps in when you have the idea that you are to be 'a written epistle' — of course you are! but you have not to know it.

Whenever you meet a man who is going on with God you find his testimony explains your own experience. A true testimony grips everyone who is after the Truth.

It is easier to stand true to a testimony mildewed with age, because it has a dogmatic ring about it that people agree with, than to talk from your last moment of contact with God.

Am I trying to live up to a testimony, or am I abiding in the Truth?

The danger of experience-meetings when they get outside the New Testament standard is that people don't testify to anything that glorifies God, but to experiences that leave you breathless and embarrassed. It is all on the illuminated line, on the verge of the hysterical.

People are precipitated into testifying before the vision they have had is made real — 'Now I have had this experience,' or, 'Now I have become that.' What we need to do after the vision is to examine ourselves before God and see if we are willing for all that must happen before it is made real in us.

When we get the vision of what God wants us to be, we are put to the blush by what we actually are, and that humiliation is the precursor of the coming reality, a heart-panging disgust at the realisation of what I am. That is what the Holy Spirit works in me; a disgust that will end in nothing less than death, then God can begin to make the vision real.

Never give an educated testimony, ie., something you have taught yourself to say; wait till the elemental moves in you.

Be prepared to be unreserved in personal testimony; but remember, personal testimony must never be lowered into personal biography.

You cannot bring a knowledge of Jesus Christ to another, you can only tell him what He is to you, but until he gets where you are he will never see what you see.

If my testimony makes anyone wish to emulate me, it is a mistaken testimony, it is not a witness to Jesus.

The Holy Spirit will only witness to a testimony when Jesus Christ is exalted higher than the testimony.

TWENTY

THINKING

'*F*OR WHO AMONG men knoweth the things of a man, save the spirit of the man, which is in him?' A man discovers intellectual things for himself but he cannot discover God by his intellect. '…even so the things of God none knoweth, save the Spirit of God' (1 Cor 2:11).

Think of the labour and patience of men in the domain of science and then think of our lack of patience in endeavouring to appreciate the Atonement, and you see the need there is for us to be conscientious in our thinking, basing everything on the reality of the Atonement. We prefer to be average Christians, we don't mind it having broken God's heart to save us, but we do object to having a sleepless night while we learn to say 'Thank you' to God so that the angels can hear us. We need to be staggered out of our shocking indolence.

We have no business to limit God's revelations to the bias of the human mind.

'I can't alter my thinking.' You can. It is actually possible to identify your mind with the highest point of view, and to habituate yourself by degrees to the thinking and the living in accordance with it.

A man's mental belief will show sooner or later in his practical living.

If I make my life in my intellect I will certainly

delude myself that I am as good as I think I am. 'As a man thinketh *in his heart*' — that means 'me', as I express my thinking in actual life, *'so is he'*.

I can think out a whole system of life, reason it all out well, but it does not necessarily make any difference to my actual life, I may think like an angel and live like a tadpole.

Note the things your thinking does not account for.

Truth is discerned by moral obedience. There are points in our thinking which remain obscure until a crisis arises in personal life where we ought to obey, immediately we obey the intellectual difficulty alters. Whenever we have to obey it is always in something immensely practical.

Obedience is the basis of Christian thinking. Never be surprised if there are whole areas of thinking that are not clear, they never will be until you obey.

Every new domain into which your personal life is introduced necessitates a new form of responsible intelligence.

Watch what you say you don't understand — you understand only too clearly.

Learn to be glad when you feel yourself a chaos that makes you bitterly disappointed with yourself, because from that moment you will begin to understand that God alone can make you 'order' and 'beauty'.

Young life must be in chaos or there is no development possible.

Until you get an answer that satisfies your best moods only, don't stop thinking, keep on querying God. The answers that satisfy you go all over you, like health, or fresh air.

Don't shut up any avenue of your nature, let God come into every avenue, every relationship, and you will find the nightmare curse of 'secular and sacred' will go.

Intellectual obstinacy produces the sealed mind — 'Jesus said unto them, If ye were blind, ye would have no sin: but now ye say, We see: your sin remaineth' (Jn 9:41, RV).

There is no jump into thinking, it is only done by a steady determined facing of the facts brought by the engineering of circumstances. God always insists that I think *where I am.* Beware of that abortion of Providence — 'If I were you,...'

With regard to other men's minds, take all you can get, whether those minds are in flesh-and-blood editions or in books, but remember, the best you get from another mind is not that mind's verdict, but its standpoint. Note the writers who provoke you to do your best mentally.

Never cease to think until you think things home and they become character.

Very few of us are real as God is real, we are only real in spots — awake morally and spiritually and dead intellectually, or *vice versa*, awake intellectually and dead morally and spiritually. It takes the shaking of God's Providence to awaken us up as whole beings, and when we are awakened we get growing pains in moral senses, in spiritual muscles we have never used. It is not the devil, it is God trying to make us appreciative sons and daughters of His.

Our thinking is often allowed to be anti-Christian while our feelings are Christian. The way I think will colour my attitude towards my fellow-men.

Always make a practice of provoking your mind to think about what it easily accepts. A position is not yours until you make it yours through suffering.

If you have ever done any thinking you don't feel very complacent after it, you get your first touch of pessimism; if you don't, you have never thought clearly and truly.

An appalling thing is that men who ignore Jesus Christ have their eyes open in a way many a preacher of the Gospel has not. Ibsen, for instance, saw things clearly: he saw the inexorable results of sin but without any deliverance or forgiveness, because he saw things apart from the Atonement.

The first thing that goes when you begin to think is your theology. If you stick too long to a theological point of view you become stagnant, without vitality.

Never try to pillory Incarnate Reason by your own petty intelligence.

'I have yet many things to say unto you, but ye cannot bear them now' (Jn 16:12, RV). These words are true in our mental life as well as in our spiritual life.

Doubt is not always a sign that a man is wrong; it may be a sign that he is thinking.

Keep the powers of your mind going full pace, always maintaining the secret life right with God.

If you teach anything out of an idle intellect, you will have to answer to God for it.

Never be distressed at the immediate result of thinking on the deep truths of religion because it will take years of profound familiarity with such truths before you gain an expression sufficient to satisfy you.

God never simply gives us an answer, He puts us on a line where it is possible for Truth to break more and more as we go on.

Before the mind has begun to grapple with problems it is easy to talk; when the mind has begun to grapple with problems it is a humiliating thing to talk.

Unless you think, you will be untouched, unbroken, by the truths you utter.

A logical position is satisfying to intellect, but it can never be true to life. Logic is simply the method man's intellect follows in making things definable to himself, but you can't define what is greater than yourself.

We command what we can explain, and if we bring our explanation into the spiritual domain we are in danger of explaining Jesus away — 'and every spirit which annulleth Jesus is not of God' (1 Jn 4:3, RV marg). We have to be intelligently more than intelligent, intellectually more than intellectual, that is, we have to use all our wits in order not to worship our wits but be humble enough to worship God.

Don't run away with the idea that everything that runs contrary to your complacent scheme of things is of the devil.

As you go on with God He will give you thoughts that are a bit too big for you. God will never leave a servant of His with ideas he can easily express, He will always express through him more than he can grasp.

It takes a long time to get rid of atheism in thinking.

WORKERS FOR GOD

THE WORKER FOR God must live among the common-sense facts of the natural world, but he must also be at home with revelation facts.

Be a worker with an equal knowledge of sin, of the human heart, and of God.

Never take it for granted because you have been used by God to a soul that God will always speak through you, He won't. At any second you may blunt your spiritual intuition, it is known only to God and yourself. Keep the intuitive secret life clear and right with God at all costs.

Never pray for the gift of discernment, live so much in contact with God that the Holy Spirit can point out through you to others where they are wrong.

Our confidence is to be based on the fact that it is God who provides the issue in lives; we have to see that we give Him the opportunity of dealing with men by ceasing to be impressive individuals.

Beware of allowing the discernment of wrong in another to blind you to the fact that you are what you are by the grace of God.

How do I deal with a sinful soul? do I remember who I am, or do I deal with him as if I were God?

Never say, 'That truth is applicable to So-and-so,' it puts you in a false position. To know that the truth is applicable to another life is a sacred trust from God to you, you must never say anything about it. Restraint in these matters is the way to maintain communion with God.

How many people have you made homesick for God?

The value of our work depends on whether we can direct men to Jesus Christ.

'Lovest thou Me?' 'Feed My sheep.' That means giving out my life-blood for others as the Son of God gave His life-blood for me.

Christian service is not our work; loyalty to Jesus is our work.

Whenever success is made the motive of service infidelity to our Lord is the inevitable result (cf Luke 10:20).

The curse of much modern Christian work is its determination to preserve itself.

This fundamental principle must be born in mind, that any work for God before it fulfils its purpose must die, otherwise it 'abides alone'. The conception is not that of progress from a seed to full growth, but of a seed dying and bringing forth what it never was. That is why Christianity is always 'a forlorn hope' in the eyes of the world.

The element of faith that enables us to experience salvation is less than the faith required to make us workers for God. We have to bring into harmony all the strayed forces of our nature and concentrate them on the life of faith.

Beware of the temptation to compromise with the world, to put their interests, their needs, first — 'They have kindly become interested in our Christian work, given so much time to it, now let us winsomely draw them in' — they will winsomely draw you away from God.

We constantly ask, 'Am I of any use?' If you think

you are, it is questionable whether you are being used by the Holy Spirit at all. It is the things you pay no attention to that the Holy Spirit uses.

Your dead-set determination to be of use never means half so much as the times you have not been thinking of being used — a casual conversation, an ordinary word, while your life was 'hid with Christ in God'.

As a worker, you must know how to link yourself on to the power of God; let the one you are talking to have the best of it for a time, don't try to prove that you are in the right and he is in the wrong. If we battle for a doctrinal position we will see no further spiritually.

Never interfere with God's providential dealings with other souls. Be true to God yourself and watch.

Individual responsibility for others without becoming an amateur providence, is one of the accomplishments of the Holy Spirit in a saint.

As workers for God, feed you heart and mind on this truth, that as individuals we are mere iotas in the great purpose of God. Every evangelical 'craze' is an attempt to confine God to our notions, whereas the Holy Spirit constrains us to be what God wants us to be.

The greatest service you can render God is to fulfil your spiritual destiny.

Where would you be if God took away all your Christian work? Too often it is our Christian work that is worshipped and not God.

We rush through life and call ourselves practical, we mistake activity for real life, consequently when the activity stops we go out like a vapour, it has not been based on the great fundamental energy of God.

'Beware of Christian *activities* instead of Christian

being. The reason workers come to stupendous collapses is that their work is the evidence of a heart that evades facing the truth of God for itself — 'I have no time for prayer, for Bible study, I must be always at it.'

The lives that are getting stronger are lives in the desert, deep-rooted in God; they always remind you of God whenever you come in contact with them.

Never shrink from dealing with any life you are brought up against, but never go unless you are quite sure God wants you to, He will guide. God's permission means there is no shadow of doubt on the horizon of consciousness; when there is, wait. God never guides by fogs or by lightning flashes, He guides naturally.

Don't insult God by despising His ordinary ways in your life by saying, 'Those things are beneath me.' God has no special line, anything that is ordinary and human is His line.

Any worker following Paul's advice to Timothy — 'Preach the word; be instant in season, out of season,...' (2 Tim 4:2) will be continually surprised with new discoveries of truth, and there will be a perennial freshness about the spoken word.

You cannot be too severe with self-pity in yourself or in others. Be more merciless with yourself than you are with others.

Remember, weariness in work which is attended by spiritual weakness means you have been using your vital energy without at the same time witnessing. Natural weariness in work while you witness, produces steady and wonderful rejuvenescence.

If you obey God His order may take you into a cesspool but you will never be hurt.

If my life as a worker is right with God I am not concerned about my public pose — using discreet terms that will impress people; my one concern in public and private is to worship God.

When a worker jealously guards his secret life with God the public life will take care of itself.

Remember, in estimating other lives there is always one fact more you don't know. You don't know why some men turn to God and others don't, it is hidden in the inscrutable part of a man's nature.

If we realize the intense sacredness of a human soul in God's sight we will no longer romp in where angels fear to tread, we will pray and wait.

Never talk for the sake of making the other person see you are in the right, talk only that he may see the right, and when he does see it you will be so obliterated that he will forget to say 'Thank you'.

Notice carefully by what you are hurt and see whether it is because you are not being obeyed, or whether it is because the Holy Spirit is not being obeyed. If it is because you are not being obeyed, there is something desperately wrong with you.

In the majority of cases we don't care a bit about a soul rebelling against Jesus Christ, but we do care about his humiliating us.

Nothing hoodwinks us more quickly than the idea that we are serving God.

The last lesson we learn is 'Hands off', that God's hands may be on.

When you are brought face to face with a case of happy indifference, pray for all you are worth, but let him alone with your tongue — the hardest thing for an earnest Christian to do.

It is much easier to do Christian work than to be concentrated on God's point of view.

Beware lest human pity pervert the meaning of Calvary so that you have more compassion for a soul than for the Saviour.

As 'workers together with God' we are called upon not to be ignorant of the forces of the day in which we live. God does not alter, the truths of the Bible do not alter, but the problems we have to face do alter.

Never allow anyone to confess to you unless it is for his own soul's sake, make him tell God. The habit of confessing tends to make one person dependent on another, and the one who confesses becomes a spiritual sponge, mopping up sympathy.

The judicious weighing of what you should allow other people to tell you and what not to allow them to tell you, depends on two things: your experience of life among men, and your experience of life with God.

Never give a soul the help God alone should give; hand him right on to God.

Keep your mind stayed on God, and I defy anyone's heart to stop at you, it will always go on to God. Our duty is to present God, and never get in the way even in thought.

My business as a worker is to see that I am living on the basis of the Atonement in my actual life.

When you come in contact with the great destructive sins in men's lives, be reverent with what you don't understand. God says, 'Leave that one to Me.'

'We then, as workers together with Him...', the One referred to is Almighty God, 'the Creator of the ends of the earth.' Think of the impregnable position it gives the feeblest saint to remember that he is a fellow-worker with God.